THE HULK WILL ALWAYS BE A PART OF DR. BRUCE BANNER, BUT BANNER WANTS TO BE REMEMBERED
OR HIS CONTRIBUTIONS TO SCIENCE AND NOT FOR TURNING INTO A BIG, GREEN FORCE OF RAGE
ND DESTRUCTION. TO ACHIEVE THAT GOAL, BANNER HAS STRUCK A MUTUALLY BENEFICIAL DEAL
ITH MARIA HILL, THE DIRECTOR OF S.H.I.E.L.D. SHE PROVIDES BANNER WITH A LAB, STAFF AND
LL OF THE RESOURCES HE NEEDS TO BETTER MANKIND, AND BANNER PROVIDES S.H.I.E.L.D. WITH
HE HULK FOR ANY MISSIONS THAT MIGHT NEED EXTRA MUSCLE.

INDESTRUCTIBLE HULK

HUMANITY BOMB

VOLUME 04

INDESTRUCTIBLE HULK VOL. 4: HUMANITY BOMB. Contains material originally published in magazine form as INDESTRUCTIBLE HULK #16, #17.INH-19.INH, #20 and ANNUAL #1. First printing 2014.
ISBN# 978-0-7851-5480-8. Published by MARVEL WORLDWIDE, INC., a subsidiary of MARVEL ENTERTAINMENT, LLC. OFFICE OF PUBLICATION: 135 West 50th Street, New York, NY 10020. Copyright ©
2013 and 2014 Marvel Characters, Inc. All rights reserved. All characters featured in this issue and the distinctive names and likenesses thereof, and all related indicia are trademarks of Marvel Characters,
Inc. No similarity between any of the names, characters, persons, and/or institutions in this magazine with those of any living or dead person or institution is intended, and any such similarity which may
exist is purely coincidental. **Printed in the U.S.A.** ALAN FINE, EVP - Office of the President, Marvel Worldwide, Inc. and EVP & CMO Marvel Characters B.V.; DAN BUCKLEY, Publisher & President - Print,
Animation & Digital Divisions; JOE QUESADA, Chief Creative Officer; TOM BREVOORT, SVP of Publishing; DAVID BOGART, SVP of Operations & Procurement, Publishing; C.B. CEBULSKI, SVP of Creator &
Content Development; DAVID GABRIEL, SVP Print, Sales & Marketing; JIM O'KEEFE, VP of Operations & Logistics; DAN CARR, Executive Director of Publishing Technology; SUSAN CRESPI, Editorial Operations
Manager; ALEX MORALES, Publishing Operations Manager; STAN LEE, Chairman Emeritus. For information regarding advertising in Marvel Comics or on Marvel.com, please contact Niza Disla, Director of
Marvel Partnerships, at ndisla@marvel.com. For Marvel subscription inquiries, please call 800-217-9158. **Manufactured between 4/4/2014 and 5/19/2014 by R.R. DONNELLEY, INC., SALEM, VA, USA.**

10 9 8 7 6 5 4 3 2 1

WRITER
MARK WAID

#16
ARTIST: **MAHMUD ASRAR**

#17
ARTISTS: **CLAY & SETH MANN**
(PGS 1-10, 12-13) AND
MIGUEL SEPULVEDA
(PGS 11, 14-20)

#18
ARTISTS: **JHEREMY RAAPACK**
(PGS 1-10) AND
MIGUEL SEPULVEDA WITH
TOM GRUMMETT (PGS 11-20)

#19
ARTISTS: **JHEREMY RAAPACK**
(PGS 1-12, 16, 19-20), **JOE BENNETT** &
RUY JOSÉ (PGS 13-15) AND
TOM GRUMMETT WITH
KARL KESEL &
ANDREW HENNESSY (PGS 17-18)

#20
PENCILER: **JOE BENNETT**
INKERS: **RUY JOSÉ** WITH
SCOTT HANNA

COLORIST: **VAL STAPLES**
LETTERER: **VC'S CORY PETIT**

ANNUAL #1
WRITER: **JEFF PARKER**
ARTIST: **MAHMUD ASRAR**
COLORIST: **NELSON DANIEL**
LETTERER: **VC'S CORY PETIT**

COVER ARTISTS: **MAHMUD ASRAR**
& **DAVE MCCAIG**

ASSISTANT EDITOR: **EMILY SHAW**
EDITOR: **MARK PANICCIA**

COLLECTION EDITOR: **ALEX STARBUCK** • EDITORS, SPECIAL PROJECTS: **JENNIFER GRÜNWALD & MARK D. BEAZLEY**
SENIOR EDITOR, SPECIAL PROJECTS: **JEFF YOUNGQUIST** • SVP PRINT, SALES & MARKETING: **DAVID GABRIEL**
BOOK DESIGNER: **NELSON RIBEIRO**

DITOR IN CHIEF: **AXEL ALONSO**
HIEF CREATIVE OFFICER: **JOE QUESADA**
UBLISHER: **DAN BUCKLEY**
XECUTIVE PRODUCER: **ALAN FINE**

PREVIOUSLY

AFTER DELIVERING A PUNCH STRAIGHT TO THE FACE OF TIME ITSELF,
HULK HAS SAVED THE PAST. EVERYTHING WENT BACK TO NORMAL.
FOR THE MOST PART. SOMETHING WAS CHANGED...

BUT HULK'S JAUNT THROUGH TIME MEANS BANNER IS BEHIND IN
HIS WORK.

HULK DESTROYS, BANNER BUILDS.

I...I CAN'T HELP YOU.

I CAN'T. IT'S A MATTER OF NATIONAL DEFENSE.

THE M-MONEY YOU'RE ASKING FOR...IT'S ALREADY EARMARKED AND BUDGETED.

MY SUPERIORS WOULD NOTICE IF I REROUTED IT. THERE'D BE SECURITY GRILLINGS--

LET'S TALK ABOUT SECURITY, MR....

...MR. TIPTREE.

SEE, I FEEL VERY INSECURE RIGHT NOW.

AND THAT ANNOYS ME. MAKES ME EDGY. DOWNRIGHT HOSTILE.

TIPTREE, SIMON

IT'S HOT IN HERE. IS IT HOT TO YOU...?

PAY ATTENTION TO ME WHEN I'M TALKING!

SLAM

I UNDERSTAND ALL ABOUT NATIONAL DEFENSE, SIR.

NO ONE IS ASKING YOU TO COMPROMISE THE SAFETY OF THE UNITED STATES.

BUT WE BOTH KNOW HOW MUCH PORK THERE IS IN THAT BUDGET...HOW MUCH WASTE.

AND WE BOTH KNOW THAT YOU HAVE THE POWER TO REALLOCATE MUCH OF THAT, ON THE SLY, TO MY PEOPLE WITHOUT IT BEING MISSED.

THAT'S ALL I'M ASKING YOU TO DO. MY OPERATION IS STRAPPED FOR CASH. I SUPPOSE YOU COULD SAY NO...

TUESDAY.
BRUCE BANNER'S
S.H.I.E.L.D. LAB.

WORK DIARY OF
DR. BRUCE BANNER.

"Hulk destroys, Banner BUILDS."
A great MOTTO, but lately, with
all Hulk's jaunting through TIME
and SPACE, BANNER's fallen
BEHIND on his end of that deal.

I promised myself a completed invention--
something NEW and WORLD-CHANGING--
every FRIDAY without FAIL, and I'm bound
and determined to get back on SCHEDULE.

Thanks to the new BUDGET,
I can JUST MAKE IT with THIS:
the world's first fusion-
powered HIGH-SPEED RAIL...

DOC,
YOU SHOULD
SEE THIS...

TOMORROW'S SCIENCE TODAY
TONY STARK DELIVERS
GAME-CHANGING FUSION-POWERED RAIL ENGINE

...engine...

STARRRRRK--!

AR

THURSDAY.

I've been DREAMING of getting back to THIS one.

Microminiature bloodstream vessels programmed to deposit medicine more precisely and directly in the human body.

--IT'S A LONG FLY BALL TO CENTER FIELD-- MENDOZA REACHING, REACHING, REACH

BDEEP!

Incoming call. No time for chats. I'll phone 'em back.

MESSAGE PLAYBACK:

BRUCE? BRUCE, HEY, IT'S HANK PYM! LISTEN, I WANTED A SECOND SET OF EYES ON SOMETHING IF YOU HAVE SATURDAY FREE.

I'VE CONSTRUCTED A MICROSCOPIC IMPLANT THAT CAN DELIVER MEDICINAL PAYLOADS--

JESSUP, GET DIRECTOR HILL. NOW.

ASK HER IF S.H.I.E.L.D. NEEDS MY SERVICES FOR ANYTHING THIS AFTERNOON.

LOOK, DOC, YOU'VE ALREADY BEEN WORKIN' AROUND THE CLOCK. YOU CAN TAKE A DAY OFF. WE'LL COVER FOR--

--YOU.

NOT BANNER'S SERVICES.

MINE.

NOW!

YESSIR. DIALIN'. HERE.

WHAT'S THIS?

GUM. 120 CPM--CHEWS PER MINUTE--DELIVERS ZEN CALM IN 40 SECONDS. ALABAMA REMEDY.

GET! DIRECTOR! HILL!

YESSIR, I GOT A HULK HERE. NEEDS SOME BUSY WORK ASAP, FOLLOW? CAN Y'ALL LET THE DIRECTOR KNOW--

NOW!

--LET THE DIRECTOR KNOW *NOW*?

DWEEDWEEDWEEDWEEDWEEDWEED

RED ALERT claxon? PERFECT timing.

BANNER'S LAB HOLDING. WHAT'S THIS HERE *RED ALERT*?

WE AIN'T TURNIN' TAIL, DOCTOR. FOLLOW ME.

WHY? S.H.I.E.L.D. WON'T LET US GO WITH, PERIOD.

I DON'T THINK S.H.I.E.L.D. KNOWS ABOUT *YOUR* TAKE ON LERMA'S LIGHT-BOUNCIN' CLOAK.

INVISIBILITY, ALL DONE WITH MIRRORS. YOU OUGHTA BE A *MAGICIAN.*

JESSUP...

THOSE ANCIENT *AZTECS* MIGHT'VE FOUND SOMETHIN' WORTH "LIBERATIN'" IN *RENEWABLE ENERGY. MY* FIELD, REMEMBER?

JUST BEIN' *SELFISH,* DOCTOR.

...YOU'RE A GOOD FRIEND.

JESSUP! PHONE!

TELL HER YOU AIN'T SEEN ME.

JESSUP!

TELL. HER. I. *VANISHED.*

HANK, REMEMBER THE TALK ABOUT BUILDING AN UNDERWATER *ICE WALL* TO CONTAIN THE *FUKUSHIMA* CONTAMINATION? WE COULD *TRY* THAT WITH THE *HUDSON VALLEY*...

NO, NO, NO. I'M THINKING SOME SORT OF *COUNTER-MUTAGEN* IS THE KEY.

GENGINEERED FROM *SCRATCH?* HOW IS THAT AN *EASIER FIX?*

TONY, HEAR ME OUT. THIS CONDITION IS *GENETICALLY TRIGGERED,* RIGHT?

SO IF WE CAN *CONDENSE* THE SOLUTION TO *THAT SIZE*--

GET OUT.

BOTH OF YOU.

YOU PROMISED ME 24 HOURS!

WE'RE ON FUZZY TIME.

IS THAT A CRACK?

IT'S AN ACKNOWLEDGMENT OF HOW MUCH IS AT STAKE. DR. BANNER, I'M SURE YOU KNOW DR. MCCOY. HE HAS A GENETICS ANGLE TO ADD TO WHATEVER SPIT-AND-BALING-WIRE SOLUTION YOU'VE--

DR. HANK MCCOY OF THE X-MEN. I KNOW I SPEAK ON BEHALF OF ALL BANNER'S ASSISTANTS WHEN I SAY WHAT AN HONOR IT IS TO MEET YOU.

DR. WOLMAN, I'VE PERUSED YOUR DOCTORATE. EXEMPLARY WORK.

BRUCE, WE ARE READY TO SHOW THE WORK. WHY DON'T YOU TAKE A SEAT?

Because I don't like being reminded in front of my PEERS that I'm made of GLASS.

My crew's trying to ease the tension, but all they're doing is feeding my RESENTMENT.

Shake it off, Bruce. This is your big chance to finally SEE the respect that you've earned from these men a hundred times OVER.

They'll NEVER look at you with condescension after this.

I'M STILL THE RINGMASTER AROUND HERE, THANKS. RANDALL, ARE THE PROPULSION UNITS FUELED?

ANOTHER 10 MINUTES.

GOOD ENOUGH. GENTLEMEN, HERE'S WHAT I'VE COME UP WITH:

FOLLOW THAT BOMB!

DAMN IT, TONY, WHY DO YOU *ALWAYS* HAVE TO POKE THE *BEAR...*?

THEY DIDN'T EVEN ASK WHAT IT WAS DESIGNED TO *AFFECT!* WE HAVE TO *DO* SOMETHING!

I KNOW. WE'LL BREAK OUT OF A S.H.I.E.L.D. LOCKDOWN, RESCUE THE *BOMB* FROM THE *HULK*, THE *BEAST*, *IRON MAN* AND *PYM*--

--WRITE AN *OPERA*, TAKE A *NAP*, AND WIN THE *SUPER BOWL*. WHO'S IN?

QUITTERS.

TEACHER'S PET...

OKAY. "PENDING C-47" IS S.H.I.E.L.D.-SPEAK FOR--

--OH, WOW--

--FOR *"TERRIGEN-POSITIVE."* EVIDENTLY, AT LEAST ONE OF US HAS THE GENE THAT MAKES US SUSCEPTIBLE TO *PHYSICAL TRANSFORMATION* UPON *EXPOSURE*.

BRUCE *NEEDS* THIS, AND YOU KNOW WHAT'S AT *STAKE*!

FIRST STEP: EXIT. WHY ARE WE CONFINED, AGAIN, MELINDA?

HUH.

DOES IT SAY *WHICH* ONE?

FIVE SUITS IS *THREE HUNDRED DOLLARS*, FRANK.

THAT CLEANS ME OUT, BOBBY. YOU CAN'T DO ANY BETTER FOR AN OLD FRIEND?

MAN CAN'T PUT A PRICE ON HIS FAMILY'S *SAFETY*, FRANK. THOSE'RE GUARANTEED FOR 90 DAYS.

I'LL TAKE *FIVE.* NO-- *SIX.*

YES, SIR. JAMAL, CHECK IN THE BACK FOR SIX *LARGE.*

FRANK--

--FRANK, THESE AIN'T NOTHIN' BUT *PAINTERS' COVERALLS!* YOU'RE TAKIN' THESE FOLKS!

I AM GIVIN' THEM PEACE OF MIND, JAMAL! LOOK HOW MUCH BETTER THEY ALL FEEL!

THEY'RE *SCARED,* YOU OLD *SWINDLER!*

OF *WHAT?* OF ANOTHER GOVERNMENT *CONSPIRACY* TO KEEP US *COWED?* THAT'S ALL THIS IS!

JAMAL, AIN'T *NOBODY* GOT ANYTHING TO BE *AFRAID* OF!

TH BOOM

HULK'S HEADED RIGHT FOR YOU AND THERE'S NO WAY FOR ME TO BLOCK! ALL I CAN DO IS RISK DETONATING A BOMB OF UNKNOWN EFFECT, AND THAT'S UNACCEPTABLE!

HE'S GOING TO PUNCH THROUGH YOU LIKE A LIVING BULLET! FIRE AT WILL!

FIRE WHAT? I CAN'T EVEN STEER! WE'RE DEAD IN THE AIR--

--MOSTLY BECAUSE YOU HAD TO GO AND MAKE BANNER FEEL SMALL!

ME? I'M NOT THE ONE WHO CONCOCTED A MYSTERY EXPLOSIVE!

TONY--

--WHAT IF IT WORKS?

WHAT?

BANNER WAS RIGHT, TONY! WE WERE ARROGANT!

THAT MAN IS RECKLESS, BUT HE CAN BE BRILLIANT! WE NEVER EVEN BOTHERED TO EVEN LEARN WHAT HIS PLAN WAS! WE SIMPLY REACTED OFF YEARS OF MISTRUST!

DETONATING A RADIOACTIVE DEVICE OF UNKNOWN POTENTIAL SOUNDS INSANE--BUT WHAT IF IT WORKS?

"TONY, YOU'VE KNOWN BANNER BETTER AND LONGER THAN WE EVER WILL! IT'S YOUR CALL TO MAKE!

"PUT ASIDE ALL YOUR EGO AND RIVALRY AND DECIDE RIGHT NOW--"

DO YOU STAND DOWN--

--AND LET YOU DIE--

--DO YOU TRUST BRUCE BANNER ENOUGH TO RISK MANKIND'S SURVIVAL?

SHOOM

SHOOM

FWOOSH

FWOOSH

--and GREW to colossal size. With a BROKEN ARM.

Bones and meat and nerves and bursae, jutting and lurching and scraping...

...imagine how THAT feels.

‹UNNH›

OW. C'MON, HANK, TOUGH IT OUT...

YOU! THIS WAY!

AAAH!

NO! DON'T MOVE! YOU CAN'T! STAY PAUSED! I NEED MORE TIME--!

STOP WHINING, HANK.

WAIT. DID YOU BREAK YOUR ARM? OKAY, YOU GET TO WHINE A LITTLE.

TIME'S GONE HAYWIRE! SOME THINGS ARE SLOWING DOWN, OTHERS ARE SPEEDING UP! WHAT NEEDS DOING?

THERE'S ABOUT A TON OF BROKEN GLASS SUSPENDED OVER THE STREET! BANNER'S BOMB MUST HAVE BLOWN EVERY WINDOW OUT--

--AND IT'S ALL GOING TO RAIN DOWN. GOT IT.

GHUH.

AAAH!

WHERE AM I? WHAT DAY IS IT?

AND WHY AM I CRASHING?

WELL THE *GOOD* NEWS IS, WE'VE THROWN OUR CAREERS AWAY FOR *NOTHING.*

S.H.I.E.L.D. SAYS DOC BANNER MADE IT *THROUGH.*

WOO-HOO!

AND HIS HULKNAPPED BOMB?

NO LIVES LOST.

YESYES YES!

WELL? ANYBODY FEEL... TERRIGEN-Y?

CAN I GET AN "ARRGH! I'M CHANGING"?

LET'S LEAVE ASIDE THE TOPIC OF PATRICIA'S PUZZLING BUT CLEARLY EVIDENT DESIRE TO CHANGE INTO A *MONSTER.*

Puzzling ONLY if you don't know her SECRET: Patricia Wolman is DYING of an incurable disease.

OUR *ORDERS* ARE TO PICK THE DOCTOR UP IN *TULSA,* HURRY BACK TO BASE, AND PRESENT OUR THROATS TO DIRECTOR HILL'S BLADE.

GETS YOU, DOESN'T IT, JESSUP?

WE PUT OUR LIVES--OUR *HUMANITY*--ON THE LINE FOR BANNER, AND THE BUREAUCRATS TREAT US LIKE *CRIMINALS?*

IT'LL WORK OUT, VETERI. HILL'S GOT TO CROSS HER T'S IS ALL.

CLASSIC JESSUP. KING OF NON-CONFRONTATION. YOU ALWAYS DO THIS.

...OMEONE TICKS YOU OFF, ...ND A CASUAL OBSERVER WOULD MISS IT. BUT ...HOSE OF US WHO *KNOW* YOU CAN SEE THE RAGE FLICKER ACROSS YOUR FACE.

THEN YOU STUFF IT DOWN AND SMILE, AND MAKE SOME LAME EXCUSE FOR WHOEVER OR WHATEVER *PROVOKED* YOU.

THINGS ARE STRESSFUL FOR ALL OF US, I *KNOW* THAT. WE WALK ON EGGSHELLS AROUND DR. BANNER 24-7, AND SOME OF THE WAYS WE *DEAL* AREN'T *IDEAL*--

HA! YOU'RE DOING IT *NOW!* EXCUSING *ME!* OH, YOU'RE A PIECE OF WORK, JESSUP.

I CAN *SEE* HOW YOU BECAME BANNER'S *PET.*

RAAAR!

KRENNCH

RANDY

Normally, SOLUTIONS are pretty STRAIGHTFORWARD. Hulk sees problem, Hulk HITS problem. But it helps to have SOME idea of what he's looking at.

DON'T BE MAD

That doesn't stop him from BLUSTERING and BULLYING--

NO CRASH PLANE!

--or ATTEMPTING to, anyway.

ZZZV

AAH!

The BEAMS, I would learn later, were as confusing to EVERYONE as they were to HULK. They didn't BURN, they didn't hurt FLESH...

...so what was their PURPOSE?

RAAAAR!

Poor JESSUP was GONE. In his place, a MONSTER.

I could FEEL for him.

URRR!

And that's when I began to WAKE UP.

Ordinarily, I don't share a CONSCIOUSNESS with Hulk. But something BIZARRE was going on.

All of the RAGE, all of the FURY that sources the Hulk's every motive force--

--it was ebbing AWAY.

Like infection from a wound.

HUH?

AAA-HA! HA!

And for the first time, the HULK fully tastes a feeling BANNER only barely REMEMBERS.

HAHA!

HAHAHAHAHAHA!

HAHAHAHA!

The ABSENCE of ANGER.

Where did it GO?

19

RANDALL JESSUP.

He was part of my team of ASSISTANTS--

--before fate and an alien substance called TERRIGEN made him an ANGER-VAMPIRE.

Transformed minutes earlier by that inhumanizing mutagen, that process ITSELF altered by an exploding WARHEAD--

--Okay, MY exploding warhead--

--he began literally to FEED on the rage of OTHERS.

CALIFORNIA. 3RD ANNUAL "CAUSE CEREBRAL" THINK TANK.

--AND FINALLY, WE LOOK TO THOSE LATE SCIENTIFIC INNOVATORS WHO TOILED IN THE SECRET LAB CODE-NAMED "*BEEHIVE*"--

--AND TO THE TRANSFORMATIONAL CHALLENGES THOSE CHANGE-AGENTS MODELED FOR THOUGHT-LEADERS TO COME.

DID THE BEEHIVE EXIST IN RUMOR OR IN FACT?

DID AN ENCLAVE OF SCIENCE-ENTREPRENEURS SECRETLY DEVELOP A HUMAN UPGRADE?

DID THAT SENTIENT BREAKTHROUGH EMERGE FROM ITS COCOON AND DELETE ITS MAKERS IN A PASSION OF CREATIVE DESTRUCTION?

THE ANSWER IS, IT DOESN'T *MATTER*. FACTS *DIE*, BUT *IDEAS* BREATHE *FOREVER*...

...AND NEW *COCOONS* MATERIALIZE EVERY DAY.

BRAVO!

ENCORE!

CLAPCLAPCLAPCLAPCLAPCLAPCLAP

DR. GOODRICH! HOW DID IT **GO?**

I DEMATERIALIZED TO DEAFENING **CHEERS,** DR. WEBB. EVEN NOW, THE STUNNED PRINCES OF **SILICON VALLEY** ARE **SCRAMBLING** TO CLICK ON OUR **"DONATE"** BUTTON.

SUCCESS, THEN.

YOU CAN NEVER LOSE BY PRESSING MEANINGLESS BUZZWORDS INTO THE SERVICE OF **WISHFUL THINKING.** A **DREAM** IS AN **EASY SELL.**

BUT DON'T EXPECT TO **STALL** ME WITH **SMALL TALK.** I AWAIT YOUR REPORT ON THE CONDITION OF OUR **GUEST.**

ALL OF THOSE **SERMONS** ABOUT "INNOVATION," AND YOU'RE SECRETLY AS SINCERE AS A MASS-MARKET **GREETING CARD.**

I BELIEVE THE BEEHIVE **EXISTED,** AND THAT THE ENCLAVE WERE ONTO SOMETHING **HUGE.** I BELIEVE WE CAN **PROFIT** FROM HAVING UNEARTHED THEIR FACILITY.

AND I BELIEVE YOU'D **BETTER** ANSWER MY QUESTION.

SCANS DETECT A NEGLIGIBLE RATE OF CHANGE IN THE CONDITION OF THE CAPTURED TERRIGEN COCOON DESPITE OUR BEST EFFORTS.

LASERS ARE PENETRATING AT A RATE OF ONLY 11 MICROMETERS PER HOUR. ADAMANTIUM SCRAPING YIELDS SIMILAR RESULTS, AS DO SUSTAINED ACID BLASTS.

UNACCEPTABLE.

INTELLECTUALLY, I REALIZE IT'S UNFOUNDED, DR. BANNER. THAT IT'S NOT HIS FAULT. BUT MY GUT CAN'T LET IT GO. I SEE JESSUP AND I WANT TO...

...SMASH HIS FACE, HONESTLY, I DO.

BECAUSE HE MUTATED AND YOU DIDN'T.

BECAUSE I'M THE ONE WHO *NEEDED* TO MUTATE.

I LOST THE LOTTERY WHEN I GOT THIS STUPID DISEASE, AND I LOST IT AGAIN WHEN TERRIGEN PICKED RANDY JESSUP AND NOT *ME*. I CAN'T KEEP LOSING.

RANDALL *ABSORBS* ANGER AS AN *ENERGY*, PATTY. THAT'S WHAT *TRANSFORMS* HIM. NEXT TIME, THE CHANGE COULD BE *PERMANENT*. WE ALL HAVE TO WATCH OUR MOODS.

YOU AND I, *ESPECIALLY*.

AND IF WE PULL IT OFF, DOCTOR? IF WE TIPTOE AND WHISPER AND HE STAYS THE WAY HE IS?

YOU EXAMINED HIM THOROUGHLY, RIGHT? IS THERE ANY CHANCE WE FIND A CURE?

I THINK I ALREADY *HAVE*.

HOW ARE YOU FEELING, RANDY? YOU LOOK WEAKER. CAN YOU STILL TALK?

NO? OKAY. JUST LISTEN.

IT'S ODD THE WAY YOUR TRANSFORMATION KIND OF RHYMES WITH MINE. TEMPORARILY REVERSIBLE, ANGER-BASED. YOU'RE NOT LIKE OTHER TERRIGEN CASES.

I THINK THAT MIGHT BE BECAUSE YOU WERE AT GROUND ZERO WHEN WE SET OFF THE ANTI-TERRIGEN *WARHEAD.* WE'RE A COUPLE OF *BOMB BABIES,* YOU AND I.

I *THEORIZE* THAT IF WE CAN KEEP YOU STILL AND CALM OVER THE NEXT FEW HOURS...

...THIS CHRONO-PARTICLE SOLUTION HAS A *CHANCE* TO REVERSE THE MUTATION.

TO THAT END, I'LL ALSO GIVE YOU A *SEDATIVE--*

Years ago, a team of scientists toiled to create new life in a secret lab they called "THE BEEHIVE."

"Anything in the name of SCIENCE" should have been their motto. They stopped at nothing, even KIDNAPPING, in their quest.

They SUCCEEDED, and it KILLED them.

Cut to roughly the PRESENT. ANOTHER underground conclave attempted to reproduce the Beehive's work in fine detail...

...right down to snatching my assistant, Randall Jessup, as I labored to cure his life-threatening condition.

ALL OF OUR SENSORS SCREAM THAT YOU'RE LOADED WITH TERRIGEN, YET NO MUTATING EFFECT IS APPARENT. ANYTHING YOU CAN TELL ME ABOUT--

IS THAT A TRANSFER GRID?

I'VE BEEN READING ABOUT THOSE FOR YEARS. BEEHIVE, RIGHT? THE JOURNALS CAN'T SPECULATE ENOUGH.

DOES THE TELEPORT TRIGGER STILL REQUIRE SUBJECTS TO BE IN RECTILINEAR MOTION?

YOU SPEAK PHYSICS. I'M STUNNED.

ME, TOO. I DIDN'T EXPECT TO BE ABDUCTED FROM A SICKBED.

YOU'RE NOT SICK, MY FRIEND.

YOU'RE UPGRADING.

DID--
--DID I JUST GET *THE HULK* TO BASH HIS OWN *FACE* IN?

YEAH.

AH. THINK HE REMEMBERS IT WAS *ME*?

YEAH.

WHAT THE--?

DOCTOR! I'M READING A GIANT SURGE OF *TELEPORT ENERGY*, AS IF SOMETHING WERE TRYING TO BREAK *IN*--BUT ON THE WRONG *FREQUENCY*!

WHATEVER IT IS, IT'S COMING BACK *AROUND*! BRACE--

RANDY! LISTEN TO ME!

WE HAVE TO GET YOU BACK TO THE SHIP *RIGHT NOW*, OR YOUR TRANSFORMATION REALLY *WILL BE* PERMANENT!

I MEAN IT! COME NOW!

CAN YOU *HEAR* ME?

He could. But he could also hear ME-- or rather the HULK--MISDIRECTED, headed nowhere NEAR the malfunctioning teleport grid--

--and in that moment, Randy made the irreversible choice-- to award his OWN face with less importance--

--than everyone ELSE'S.

I DON'T HAVE A SUGGESTION. I HAVE AN *ORDER*. LEUCENSTERN, YOU'RE SLY. YOU CRACKED THE TELEPORTATION CODE INTO THIS PLACE. CAN YOU REBUILD IT *SAFELY* SO THAT ONLY *YOU THREE* CAN ENTER AND LEAVE?

CAKE.

THEN YOU *DON'T* COME BACK. *NONE* OF YOU DO.

IF YOU'VE LEARNED *ANYTHING* FROM ME, IT'S HOW TO COPE WITH AND WRANGLE A MAN-MONSTER. YOU THREE NOW KNOW HOW TO *TAP-DANCE* ON EGGSHELLS WHILE SIMULTANEOUSLY ACCOMPLISHING *BRILLIANCE*.

JESSUP *NEEDS* THAT. HE NEEDS *YOU*.

YOU HAVE *NO IDEA* WHERE THEY ENDED UP?

HOW MANY TIMES ARE YOU GOING TO ASK ME THAT? WHY WOULD I *LIE*?

IF YOU GO BACK TO S.H.I.E.L.D., MARIA HILL WILL *RUIN* YOU FOR DISREGARDING QUARANTINE. SO YOU STAY *HERE*. WITH JESSUP. HELP *HIM*.

BUT *YOU* NEED US.

GUYS...

...I'LL BE *FINE*.

COMPUTER, OPEN FILE "BANNER JOURNAL." PASSWORD "SMASHTONY."

BIP

RECORD.

BIP

WELL, *THAT* TOOK SOME SKIN WITH IT.

WHEN JESSUP...

...WHEN JESSUP'S PACIFYING INFLUENCE WEARS OFF, I'LL PROBABLY BE *VERY ANGRY* WITH MYSELF.

BUT IT'S TIME TO FIND A NEW PATH.

JESSUP BECOMES A MONSTER *BECAUSE* HE BROKE QUARANTINE TO LOOK FOR ME *BECAUSE* THE HULK ESCAPED...

I'M PROUD TO SAY I'VE PUT S.H.I.E.L.D. RESOURCES TO GOOD USE FOR THE WORLD. WHICH IS SURPRISING, AS I MANAGED TO IMPROVE *MYSELF* NOT AT *ALL.*

I KEEP SWEARING IT'S ALL ABOUT "HULK DESTROYS, BANNER BUILDS," BUT...

...BUT THIS *LAST* EPISODE...

...BECAUSE THE AVENGERS TRIED TO DISABLE MY BOMB *BECAUSE* I BUILT IT HASTILY... *BECAUSE I NEEDED THE CREDIT.*

ALL THOSE YEARS ON THE *RUN,* I DIDN'T GROW UP MUCH. BUT I KNOW I CAN DO *BETTER* THAN THAT.

I *WILL* DO BETTER.

FROM HERE ON OUT, I LEAVE THE *JEALOUSY* AND THE *BITTERNESS* ALL *BEHIND* ME.

STARTING NOW.

TO BE CONTINUED IN HULK #1!

I LIKE TO CONCLUDE ON A HARSH NOTE SO MY TALKS STICK.

OXFORD
FORWARD THOUGHT CONFERENCE

EVENING LECTURE

DR. DERENIK ZADIAN

HA HAHHA HAHA HAHHA HA HA

YOU STUDENTS WERE INVITED TO THIS FORUM BECAUSE YOU'RE THE BRIGHTEST OF THE BRIGHT.

YOU'VE ALL HEARD THAT ALL YOUR LIFE, AND IT'S *NOT* GOING TO DO YOU ANY FAVORS.

BECAUSE *BRILLIANT* IS ONE THING AND *FUNDED* IS ANOTHER. THEY DON'T INTERSECT AS OFTEN AS YOU'D HOPE.

THIS IS THE POINT IN YOUR LIFE WHERE YOU NEED TO DECIDE. DO YOU WANT TO BE A THEORETICIAN, WITH PROFESSORS *DEBATING YOUR RELEVANCE* DECADES AFTER YOUR DEATH?

OR DO YOU WANT TO BE A WORKING SCIENTIST TESTING YOUR IDEAS AND CHANGING THE WORLD *RIGHT NOW?*

LOOK BEHIND ME. THE PERFECT EXAMPLE.

AMERICA WAS SO TERRIFIED OF LOSING THE SPACE RACE TO RUSSIA, ANY SCIENTIST WITH SOMETHING TO OFFER ON SPACE TRAVEL HAD WORK.

THE COLD WAR WAS PERFECT. ALL OF THE FUNDING OF A REAL WAR WITH MORE TIME TO TEST AND ANALYZE.

HOW MANY OF DR. WERNER VON BRAUN'S V-2 ROCKETS LANDED SOUTH OF HERE IN LONDON IN WORLD WAR II--WAS HE TRIED AS A WAR CRIMINAL?

NO. HE WAS PUT IN CHARGE OF CONTINUING HIS WORK TO GET US UP *THERE.*

JOURNEY INTO SCIENCE

WITH...

HULK

THE HULK will always be a part of Dr. Bruce Banner, but Banner wants to be remembered for his contributions to science and not for turning into a big, green force of rage and destruction. To achieve that goal, Banner has struck a mutually beneficial deal with Maria Hill, the director of S.H.I.E.L.D. She provides Banner with a lab, staff, equipment and all of the resources he needs to better mankind, and Banner provides S.H.I.E.L.D. with the Hulk for any missions that might need extra muscle.

Recently Bruce discovered his assistant Patricia Wolman suffers from a degenerative disease. She placed herself in his lab - in proximity to **THE HULK** - knowing the possibility of a fatal work result that could payout life insurance for her father.

IRON MAN

TONY STARK is a technological visionary...a famous, wealthy and unparalleled inventor, with the world's most advanced and powerful suit of armor, Stark valiantly protects the innocent as an invincible bright knight known as...IRON MAN"

Tony Stark has become aware of a plan devised by an Artifical Intelligence to put him on the path of arming the human race against eventual extraterrestrial threat. It seems he was destined to prepare for war...

REALLY THOUGHT WE'D HIT MORE DEFENSES AS WE GOT CLOSER. IT'S BEEN A PARK VISIT SINCE WE GOT PAST THE BEACH.

YEAH, IT HAS BEEN.

TOO EASY--

WE'VE BEEN WALKING UP A NATURAL PATH-- BUT THERE ARE NO TRAIL-MAKING ANIMALS ON THIS ISLAND.

I HAVEN'T EVEN TRIPPED OVER A ROOT. IT'S LIKE THE JUNGLE IS ACCOMMODATING US!

IF THAT'S SO, IT COULD PICK A BETTER PLACE TO DUMP US. DEAD END.

MAYBE I'M JUST BEING PARANOID, BUT I FEEL--

--DIRECTED--

I'VE GOT YOU, DON'T WIG OUT!

THE END.

INCREDIBLE HULK #20, PAGE 7 ART BY JOE BENNETT & RUY JOSÉ

INCREDIBLE HULK #20, PAGE 8 ART BY JOE BENNETT & RUY JOSÉ

INCREDIBLE HULK #20, PAGE 13 ART BY JOE BENNETT & RUY JOSÉ

MARVEL AUGMENTED REALITY (AR) ENHANCES AND CHANGES THE WAY YOU EXPERIENCE COMICS!

TO ACCESS THE FREE MARVEL AR CONTENT IN THIS BOOK*:

1. Locate the **AR** logo within the comic.
2. Go to Marvel.com/AR in your web browser.
3. Search by series title to find the corresponding AR.
4. Enjoy Marvel AR!

*All AR content that appears in this book has been archived and will be available only at Marvel.com/AR — no longer in the Marvel AR App. Content subject to change and availability.

INDEX